JEWS IN SPORTS

by Joseph Hoffman

Illustrated by Janet Zwebner

PITSPOPANY

NEW YORK ◆ JERUSALEM

Design: Benjie Herskowitz

Published by PITSPOPANY PRESS

ISBN: 0-943706-68-8

Printed in Hungary

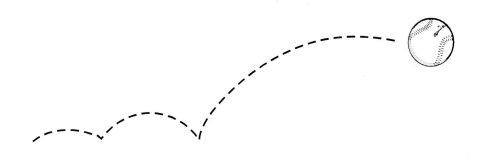

This book is dedicated to you —
The next generation of Jews in Sports!

JEWS
IN
SPORTS

INTRODUCTION

Jews have made major contributions to humanity. Moses gave us the commandments, Sigmund Freud opened up the wonders of the unconscious, and Albert Einstein unlocked the secrets of the universe.

For centuries, Jews have been known for their brain power. We have come to expect major achievements in medicine — like Jonas Salk and Albert Sabin with the elimination of polio; in law — the world famous criminal attorney and Harvard professor Alan Dershowitz; and in cinema — the highly acclaimed Steven Spielberg, to name but a few.

In the world of sports, however, the Jewish contribution is less well known. Names like baseball player Andy Cohen, sprinter Harold Abrahams, football quarterback Sid Luckman, and basketball player Dolph Schayes may be known to the professionals and sports enthusiasts, but it is only a precious few — Mark Spitz, Sandy Koufax and Hank Greenberg — who are known by the average person.

Of course these Jewish greats set records and won awards that set them apart from their Jewish *and* non-Jewish compatriots. Sandy Koufax retired after having thrown four no-hitters, the most ever at the time, and was the youngest player to be inducted into the Baseball Hall of Fame. Hank Greenberg is in a first-place tie for having hit the most home runs in a season by a right-handed batter. Mark Spitz won seven Olympic gold medals — a record still unsurpassed.

Yet, the Jewish contribution to sports is much richer and has greater depth than this handful of superstars may indicate. It started even before organized sports, way back, in the beginning of recorded history.

The Bible refers to Jacob's strength when he single-handedly moved a huge rock away from the mouth of a well, a rock the herdsmen assembled couldn't even budge. Jacob wrestled with an angel, and won! Of course he didn't get away without any wounds, and the injury to his thigh may be the first reference in literature to "hitting below the belt."

The most well-known Jewish strongman, of course, was Samson. He killed a lion with his bare hands, he tore off a city gate which was meant to have kept him prisoner, he slew 10,000 Philistines with the jawbone of a mule, and he ended his life by pulling down the Temple of Dagon.

But fairly early on, sports received a bad name in Jewish tradition. When the Greeks conquered Israel, they brought not only their military might, but their way of life as well. A big part of that life was sports. They built arenas, hippodromes (tracks for horse races) and stadiums. They encouraged Jews to compete in all sorts of sports events.

But the Jews refused to take part in Greek life, because many of the sporting events were done without clothing. This was contrary to Jewish values. Of course, there were some Jewish athletes who could not resist the lure of sports and competition and pretended to be Greeks so that they could play. There were a few that even underwent a most painful and dangerous operation to reverse the results of their circumcision so they could pass for Greek.

When the Greeks were finally overthrown by Judah Maccabee, sport was outlawed. Anything that reminded Jews of the hated Greek occupation was forbidden.

With the rise of rabbinic Judaism, many questions about the suitability of sports were raised, especially sports on Shabbat. Some rabbis said, that since sports were recreation and not work, it could be indulged in. Others, however, held that there were dangers in playing sports on Shabbat. What if equipment needed to be repaired? What if a ball broke someone's possession? Incidents like these would violate the Shabbat laws. Moreover, the spirit of Shabbat would be infringed upon, and the day that was suppose to be devoted to spiritual growth would be transformed into a day of physical enjoyment.

It was the second opinion that became the more popular, and sports were gradually looked down upon. Slowly, over the centuries, sports were replaced by an all-encompassing interest in study. Sports were considered something that Jewish children did not participate in.

This ideology lasted a long time. Then, about 150 years ago, there was an awakening of Jewish interest in sports. Jewish sporting clubs sprang up throughout Europe, capturing many honors and championships along the way.

The second great impetus to the Jewish participation in sports occurred with the birth of the State of Israel. The deskbound, pale-skinned student had to remold himself if he wanted to withstand the physical labors needed to reclaim the land of Israel. He had to build muscles *and* use his brains if he was going to build a new world.

Today, within the State of Israel, sports are thriving. Maccabi Tel Aviv basketball team has won European championships, Maccabi Tel Aviv and Maccabi Haifa have made the nation proud with their soccer exploits, and the national teams in basketball and soccer have done remarkably well abroad. The most notable of these efforts was the national soccer team's defeat of the French, which helped eliminate France from the 1992 World Cup.

Now, Jews have the freedom of choice to pursue the life of the scholar or the athlete — or, ideally, a combination of the two.

Their story is told in the following chapters, where focus is placed on great Jewish athletes who have brought fame to themselves and pride to their fellow Jews.

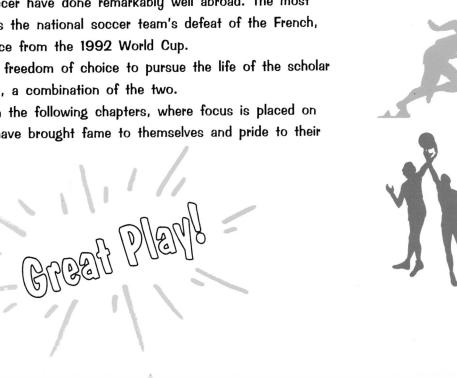

Great Play!

BASEBALL
THE EARLY YEARS

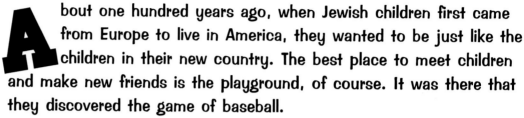

About one hundred years ago, when Jewish children first came from Europe to live in America, they wanted to be just like the children in their new country. The best place to meet children and make new friends is the playground, of course. It was there that they discovered the game of baseball.

Everyone wanted to be a baseball star. Children played in wide-open fields, empty lots and school-yards. Some even played in the street!

Jewish kids learned how to play baseball too. From the many who played in the school-yards, high schools, colleges, and the Minor Leagues, there were even a few who made it to the Big Leagues.

Here are some of their stories:

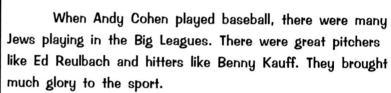

When Andy Cohen played baseball, there were many Jews playing in the Big Leagues. There were great pitchers like Ed Reulbach and hitters like Benny Kauff. They brought much glory to the sport.

The Big Leagues were a tough place then. The players were rough, and when fights started, nobody seemed to care. That's why many parents didn't want their sons to grow up in this kind of atmosphere.

Some Jews were afraid that the other players would make fun of them because they were Jewish, so they changed their names.

"What will happen if I'm not allowed to eat or sleep with the other players?" wondered first baseman Phil Cohen, who changed his name to Phil Cooney.

"What if they call us names?" asked pitcher Harry Cohen, who changed his name to Harry Kane.

"We just won't fit in," declared Al Cohen, who decided to change his name to Al King.

But for another Cohen, Andy Cohen, it was a whole different ball game.

Andy, you see, was proud to be a Jew! In fact, he became very famous because of it.

Andy was trying to become the New York Giants second baseman way back in 1926. But they already had a great second baseman — maybe even the greatest second baseman that there ever was. His name was Rogers Hornsby. Hornsby was a top player, but he didn't get along with the manager, so he was traded to the Boston Braves.

As a result, the Giants didn't have a second baseman and they sent for Andy Cohen. It was the first game of the season in New York and who do you think they were playing against that day? The Boston Braves!

Andy was scared. What if he had a bad day and all the New York fans began to shout, "What a lousy trade! Bring back Hornsby!"

Luckily, Andy had a great first game. He got two hits and scored two runs. The New York Giants beat the Boston Braves on the first day of the season. The fans in New York went wild.

The next day, all the New York newspapers showed pictures of Andy lifted up on the shoulders of his teammates. There was Andy Cohen — the hero.

He became so popular that fans wanted to change the name of the Giants stadium from Coogan's Bluff to "Cohen's Bluff."

That's not all. The supervisor of the food concessions told all his workers, "We don't sell ice cream cones anymore, we sell ice cream Cohens."

Andy also had a younger baseball-playing brother, Syd. Syd pitched for the Washington Senators for a short time. He had one great day as a pitcher; a day that everyone would remember for a long time.

The greatest player in those days was Babe Ruth. When Ruth played, he hit more home runs than any other player. Sometimes people came to the ballpark just to see Babe Ruth hit a homer. Everyone loved the Babe.

Well, it was the last game of the season and Syd Cohen and the Washington Senators were playing against Babe's New York Yankees. This was going to be Babe's last game with the Yankees and everyone wanted him to hit a home run.

Babe didn't disappoint his fans. He hit a home run off of Syd's pitch. Syd was angry at himself. "Now," he said, "everyone is going to remember me as a failure."

Syd's manager knew he was upset and was going to take him out of the game. But Syd said, "No, let me have one more chance against the Babe."

Sure enough, two innings later, there was Babe Ruth standing at the plate waiting for Syd to pitch to him.

Syd struck out the Babe. Now, people talk about Syd Cohen as the last American League pitcher to strike out Babe Ruth.

That's one reason why baseball's such a great game. A player can do poorly one inning and then get a second chance an inning later.

Jews were coming to America to start a new life — to get a second chance. Kids found that baseball was just the game for them. It gave them a second chance. It taught them to do the best that they could, and that even if they had difficulties at first, they could try again, and eventually find their place in the American way of life.

BASEBALL
THE GOLDEN AGE

Jews have always been a minority among baseball players, but that doesn't mean they haven't been famous. As a matter of fact, the greatest right-handed batter and the best left-handed pitcher were Jewish! Their names are Hank Greenberg and Sandy Koufax.

Hank Greenberg grew up in the Bronx. He was tall for his age but not particularly athletic. When he played baseball, he found that he was a natural hitter, but in the field he had problems. He wasn't fast and he had trouble getting down for ground balls.

Hank especially had trouble with his throw. It wasn't very accurate and many times his teammates were sent sprawling, trying to chase after a bad throw. The local coach went to the Greenberg home and convinced Hank's parents to allow him to set up a special drill in the backyard to sharpen Hank's throwing skills.

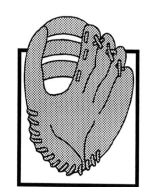

Hank's coach hung a tire from a tree. Hank was instructed to keep throwing the ball through the tire, first from a close range and, as he got better, from farther away.

Soon Hank had perfected his throw, and he joined the Detroit Tigers.

After a pretty good rookie year, Hank really caught fire. He was becoming a home run hitter — a "big stick", in the language of baseball. He led the league in home runs and RBI's (runs-batted-in) four times, and one year he almost broke Babe Ruth's single-season record of 60 home runs.

This number seemed magical. Actually, since Babe was so beloved by the American people, the fans, in particular, wanted the 60 home run record to last forever.

In 1938, Hank went on a homer-hitting streak. With another five games left to play, Hank already had 58 home runs. But suddenly Hank couldn't seem to find his range. There were some people who thought that the opposing pitchers didn't give Hank anything good to hit because they didn't want anyone breaking Ruth's mark — especially a Jew!

So when the last day of the season came around, Hank was still two home runs shy of 60. Before the game was over, however, the umpire had to call it off on account of darkness. So, Hank didn't get the chance he needed to break the Babe's record.

Hank was proud of being a Jew. He refused to play on Yom Kippur. Even though Hank's team was fighting for first place, Hank realized he couldn't let the Jewish people down by playing on this Holy Day, and he sat out the game.

Another Jewish player that became really great was Sandy Koufax.

Sandy also grew up in New York. But he played his entire career for the Dodgers. When Sandy joined the team, they were so bad at bat they were nicknamed "The Hitless Wonders". If they scored one or two runs in a game, that was a lot for them. Because of this, Sandy had to work much harder as the team's pitcher. If he gave up some runs, he stood little chance of his teammates scoring enough runs to win.

Fortunately, Sandy had a blazing fastball that gave hitters all kinds of problems. When the hitters finally figured out the fastball, Sandy would rear back and throw them the curve ball. He was close to being un-hittable.

For five straight years, Sandy led the league in the lowest number of runs given up in a game. In his career, Sandy led the league in strikeouts four times, threw four no-hitters, won three Cy Young awards (given to the best pitcher), and struck out ten batters a game on two separate occasions.

One year, the World Series opened on Yom Kippur, the Jewish Day of Atonement. Sandy, of course, was in the synagogue. So the Dodgers chose their second-best pitcher, Don Drysdale, to start. After about four innings, it was clear that Drysdale wasn't having a good game. When the manager came out on the field to put in a new pitcher, Drysdale turned to him and said, "I bet you wish I was Jewish, too, huh?"

Sandy retired at the age of thirty-one, and became the youngest player ever selected to the Hall of Fame. He joined Hank Greenberg, who had been elected to the Hall of Fame seventeen years earlier.

Batter Up!

Great Catch!

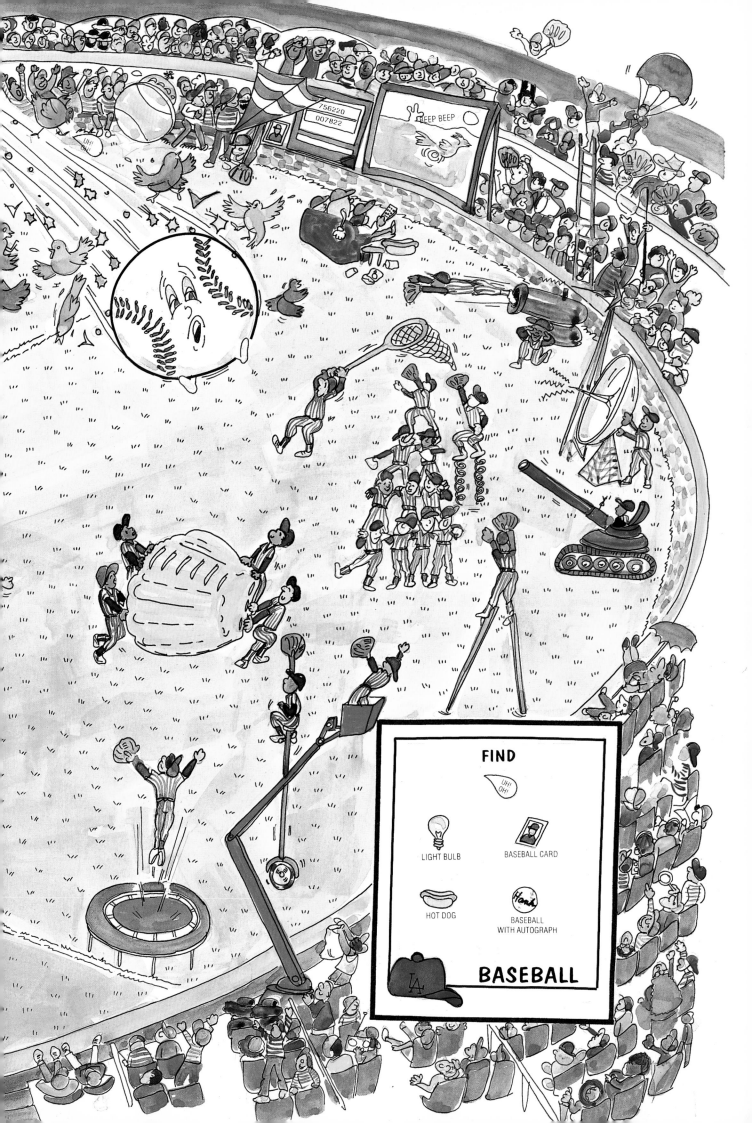

SOCCER

The most popular sport in Israel is soccer and the most popular player is Ronnie Rosenthal. For years, Ronnie was the top striker and goal scorer for Maccabi Haifa and guided the team to the national title.

Ronnie was so good that he received offers to play abroad. The rules of European soccer allow each team to have three foreign players on its team. Some of the world's greatest players have played in countries other than their own.

Ronnie recalls the day he got his first offer. "The call came just minutes before Shabbat. It was the Liverpool Soccer Club asking me to come for a tryout. I was so excited, but then I saw my mother standing behind me with a stern look on her face. I thought that she was objecting to me leaving the country. It turned out that she just wanted me to get off the phone.

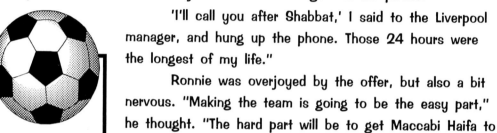

'I'll call you after Shabbat,' I said to the Liverpool manager, and hung up the phone. Those 24 hours were the longest of my life."

Ronnie was overjoyed by the offer, but also a bit nervous. "Making the team is going to be the easy part," he thought. "The hard part will be to get Maccabi Haifa to agree to the tryout."

In all professional sports, a player is under contract to a team. If Maccabi Haifa refused to let him out of his contract, Ronnie would be stuck.

But Maccabi Haifa was thrilled for Ronnie. It would be a feather in their cap if one of *their* players was selected.

"As long as he doesn't play on another team in Israel, it's fine with us," joked the Haifa manager.

So Ronnie traveled to Liverpool. He was young, inexperienced and had never left the country. "The only thing I knew about Liverpool was that it was the home of the Beatles," he quipped.

"You'll be the most important Jew in Liverpool since Brian Epstein," joked the Liverpool coach. Epstein had been the Beatles' manager before his tragic death.

Ronnie made the team. He was delighted and so was all of Israel. Ronnie was an asset to Liverpool. The style of Israeli soccer was similar to the English method, which prides itself on rough-and-tumble attacking. In Ronnie's first year with Liverpool, the club won the State Cup and came close to the league championship.

Life on the field was good for Ronnie, but off the field it was terrible. He often spent Shabbat alone while his teammates would go out of the town. "The Jewish community in Liverpool just ignored me," Ronnie laments.

Ronnie became very depressed and his game began to deteriorate. He just didn't want to stay in Liverpool. He found the courage to approach his boss and ask for a transfer.

Luckily there was a perfect place for him — the London soccer club called Tottenham Hotspur. This team is a Jewish player's heaven. It is owned by Jews, has many Jewish fans, and does not schedule games on the High Holy Days.

Ronnie was bought by Tottenham and his career began to take off.

Ronnie turned into one of the finest players on the club and regularly received standing ovations. "I get tremendous applause just by taking the field," he says. "I don't even have to play well."

Israelis love to travel and it seems like everybody wants to drop in on Ronnie. Players' phone numbers are routinely unlisted, but in Israel, Ronnie's phone number is known to all.

"My mother is so proud of me — 'My son the soccer player' — that she gives everybody my number. But only on condition that they bring me something from Israel. My apartment is filled with Israeli chocolate, newspapers, clothing — every conceivable product that the country manufactures. I should go into the import business," Ronnie jokes.

That's not a bad idea, because, as most soccer fans will tell you, Ronnie is Israel's best export.

"Life is good to me in England. I have a nice salary, a nice house and my kids go to a Jewish school. But there's nothing like coming home."

Ronnie comes home often. In the off-season, he brings his whole family and stays with his parents. During the season, he makes a number of short trips because he is still a member of Israel's national team.

"At the start of each game in Israel, I look around and see many friendly faces. When I stand at attention and listen to our national anthem, 'Hatikvah', tears come to my eyes. Then I know I'm really home."

Great Save!

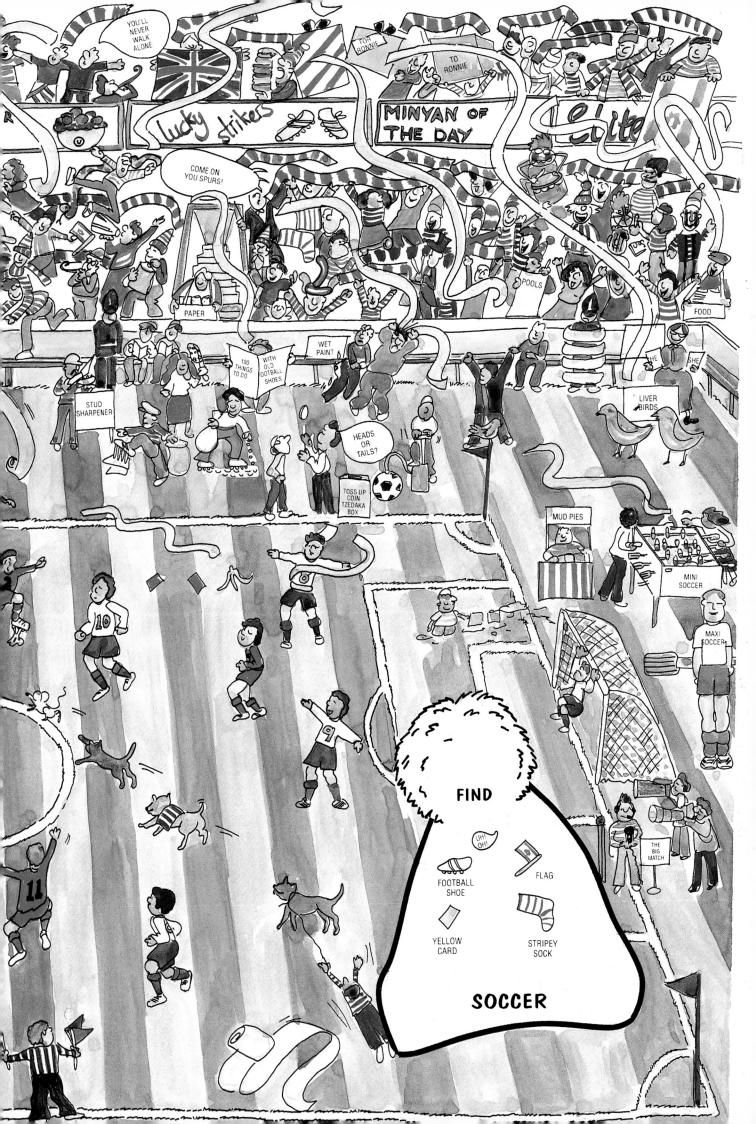

BASKETBALL

Basketball 50 years ago was hardly the sport it is today. Today you have to shoot the ball within 24 seconds, but then there was no time limit. Sometimes games were very boring with hardly a shot made, and the final score could be as low as 8-6. The game also used to be played on a screened-off court. That way, the ball could never go out of bounds. The players were always moving inside what looked like a cage. This is how the players got the nickname "cagers."

In the 1940s, however, the game underwent drastic changes due to Jewish star Dolph Schayes. Dolph grew up in the Bronx, and by ninth grade was already six-foot-five. As a sophomore at New York University, he was a towering six-foot-eight.

His size gave him an obvious advantage, but size was only part of it. Dolph developed the hard-charging style of play that we see in the NBA (National Basketball Association) today.

As a forward, one of the big offensive positions on a team, Dolph drove toward the basket so forcefully that stopping him was almost impossible. Using his height, he developed a hook shot that lifted the ball over the arms of even the tallest defenders. Dolph graduated from college as an All-American and as New York City's top player.

When he went on to the NBA, everyone thought the New York Knicks would grab him — a local star means more money at the box office. But the Knicks couldn't offer Dolph the salary he wanted, and he signed with the Syracuse Nationals.

In his first year, he was voted Rookie of the Year and led the Nats to a winning record. He had a reputation as an "iron man," playing even when injured. In nine years, Dolph played in 764 consecutive games — some with a cast on his right hand!

"That made me a better left-handed shooter," he joked.

After his playing days were over, Dolph decided to devote his time to the Jewish people and he became head coach for the United States team that went to Israel every four years for the Maccabiah Games.

"Good playing," he said, "comes from determination and smarts. You've got to know where your teammates are, what the score is, and how much time is left in the game."

Dolph is given credit for the sports phrase "You've got to keep your head in the game," meaning: you have to concentrate.

At 68-years-old, Dolph is still in great shape. The president of the United States once asked him if exercise is what keeps him fit. Dolph said, "Exercise, plus the two-handed push — away from the dinner table!"

Dolph wasn't the first or the last Jew to play in the NBA. From 1969-1977, Neil Walk played for Phoenix and the Knicks. And Doron Sheffer has become the first Israeli to be drafted by the NBA. The Los Angeles Clippers picked him as a second round draft choice, and he seems to be headed for an illustrious career.

Doron played for the University of Connecticut for three years. He was a guard, which means that he set up the plays and got all the players into their positions. A good guard is a very valuable player.

People wonder how Doron feels about living in America. "At first it was difficult," he admits. "My English wasn't so good, and it was hard to keep up with all the demands of basketball.

"But my teammates were very patient. They even tried to learn Hebrew so we could tell each other the plays without our opponents understanding.

"And I never have to worry about the High Holy Days or Passover, because there's a strong Jewish community nearby that has adopted me. Now I feel right at home."

Nadav Henefeld, another Israeli, also played at the University of Connecticut, but only for one year. He now plays in Israel for Maccabi Tel Aviv, but he helped establish the tradition of having an Israeli on Connecticut's basketball team.

While many Jews have excelled in coaching and sports administration, those in basketball have been particularly notable. The first commissioner of the National Basketball Association was a Jew named Maurice Podoloff. He was famous for securing the NBA's television contract, bringing the game into millions of households and familiarizing the American audiences with the greatest players.

Following his tradition is the NBA's present boss, David Stern. David has internationalized the NBA. He sent teams abroad to play in Japan and Germany and he encouraged Europeans to try out for NBA teams. Some of the big stars today are from Croatia, Yugoslavia and Nigeria — and one day soon — maybe from Israel, too.

A Triple Double!

TENNIS

Tennis is a lonely game. Ask any professional. As soon as one match ends, it's off to another, usually resting at some hotel and feeling all alone. That was the case with Israel's top tennis pro, Amos Mansdorf.

Mansdorf learned the game at his home in Tel Aviv. "When I first started playing, it was in school-yards after school.

"Once, my friend and I snuck onto a hotel court," Amos confesses. "We played until the guards threw us out."

Not long after, the first professional tennis courts were built in Ramat Hasharon, Israel. It had two purposes. The first was for enjoyment and the second was to produce a champion.

The tennis authorities discovered Amos and he started developing his skills. Amos remembers the first time he met Shlomo Glickstein, a top tennis pro, who was to be his trainer.

"I was so cocky," Amos recalls. "I thought I knew everything and didn't need training."

This attitude almost ended Amos' career.

"Not only did I have to train him to be a top player," says Shlomo, "I also had to get rid of his bad attitude. Amos was a real pain. He kept asking to play for money. Finally I threw down ten shekels and said, 'If you beat me, you can keep it.' Of course I won," smiles Shlomo.

When Amos turned professional, Shlomo gave him two gifts: a brand-new tennis racket and a piece of advice.

"At first, you're going to lose a lot. Don't let it get you down. Just move on to the next match."

Amos competed in about 25 matches a year. "I tried to arrange a few in the same area so I could get used to the time difference and the climate. Sometimes I was away from my family for a month," he recalls.

The toughest time to be alone was Shabbat. Amos once looked in the phone book until he found a Jewish name and called out of the blue. He often ate Shabbat dinner with people he had telephoned an hour before.

A harder problem was not playing on Shabbat. "There were games I had to forfeit," laments Amos, "because I wouldn't play on Shabbat. Some organizers were understanding and scheduled my games for other days. Some just said 'tough luck, kid.'"

But the saddest thing, Amos says, is losing in the first round. "You come to a tournament expecting to stay a long time. If you lose right away, you have lots of extra time." It's like being dressed up with nowhere to go.

Mansdorf knows what he's talking about. He was on tour for 12 years, since age 17, before he retired.

His biggest achievement was winning the Newsweek Tournament in Washington D.C. in 1993.

"My rating soared to 24th in the world," he says proudly. "Being that close to the top makes you want to play even harder."

Does Amos have any advice for youngsters just beginning their careers?

"The first thing to learn is that you are alone out there. All the good and bad shots are your responsibility.

"The second thing is to control your temper. The game is fast, and referees make mistakes. If you start yelling, you'll be slapped with a fine and no one will invite you to play."

Amos was especially proud to play on Israel's Davis Cup team which played against other countries and scored some impressive victories because of Amos.

Today, there are a new crop of tennis hopefuls. At the top of the list is Israel's best female tennis player, Anna Smashnova.

Anna's life was different from Amos'. She was born in the Soviet Union and came on aliya at age 12.

In the Soviet Union, athletes received special treatment. They were trained at the state's expense and given the finest equipment, coaches and facilities.

"The whole idea," Smashnova says, "was to create a champion. I was given the best training, but didn't have any fun. There was always pressure to succeed." Her trainers told her that if she didn't win, she would be dropped from the program. "I was afraid my classmates would make fun of me," Anna adds.

That all changed when Anna moved to Israel. She became a celebrity. She has a hard serve and volley, plays aggressively and is a rising star.

Her biggest triumph came at Wimbledon in 1994. She beat the top American player in the first round and went all the way to the quarter-finals before she lost to Steffi Graf, the best woman player in the world.

"That win won't be my biggest," Anna says with self-confidence. "I'm young, and I'm going all the way."

With a name like Smashnova, you just know she'll be a smashing success.

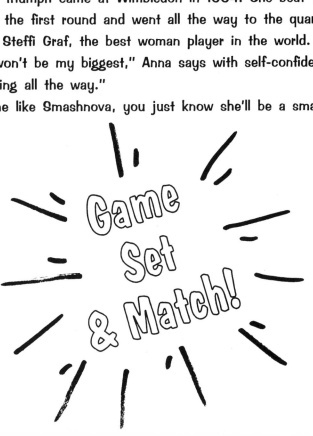

Game
Set
& Match!

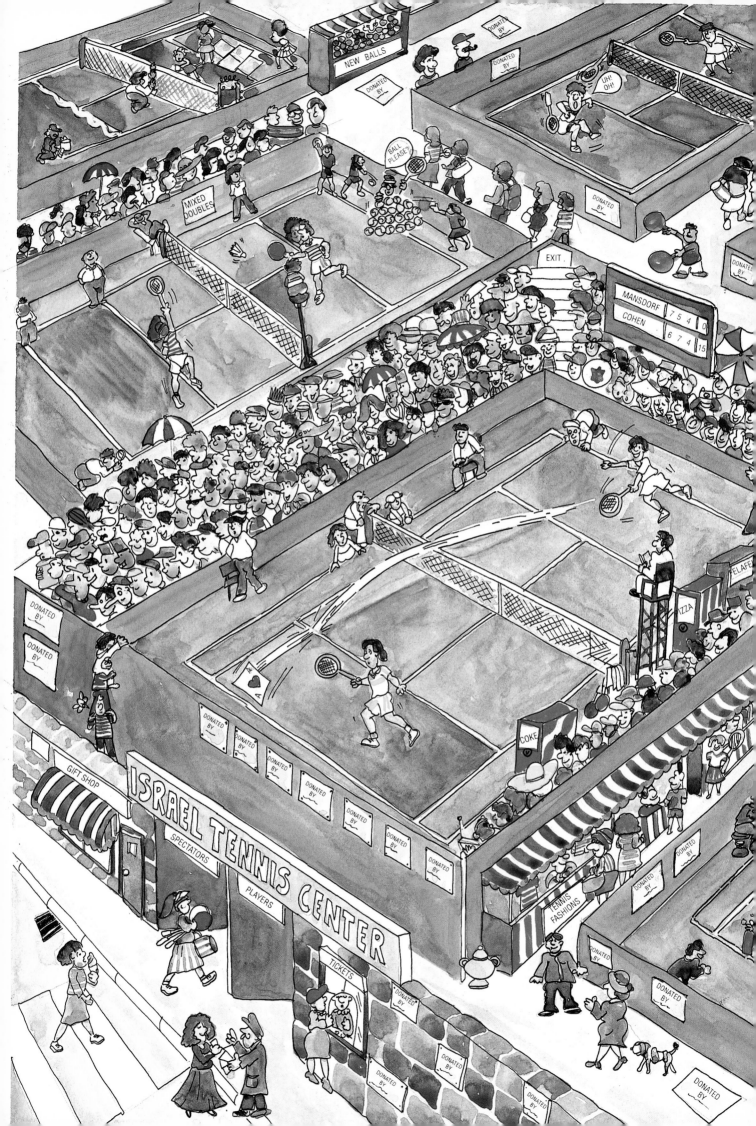

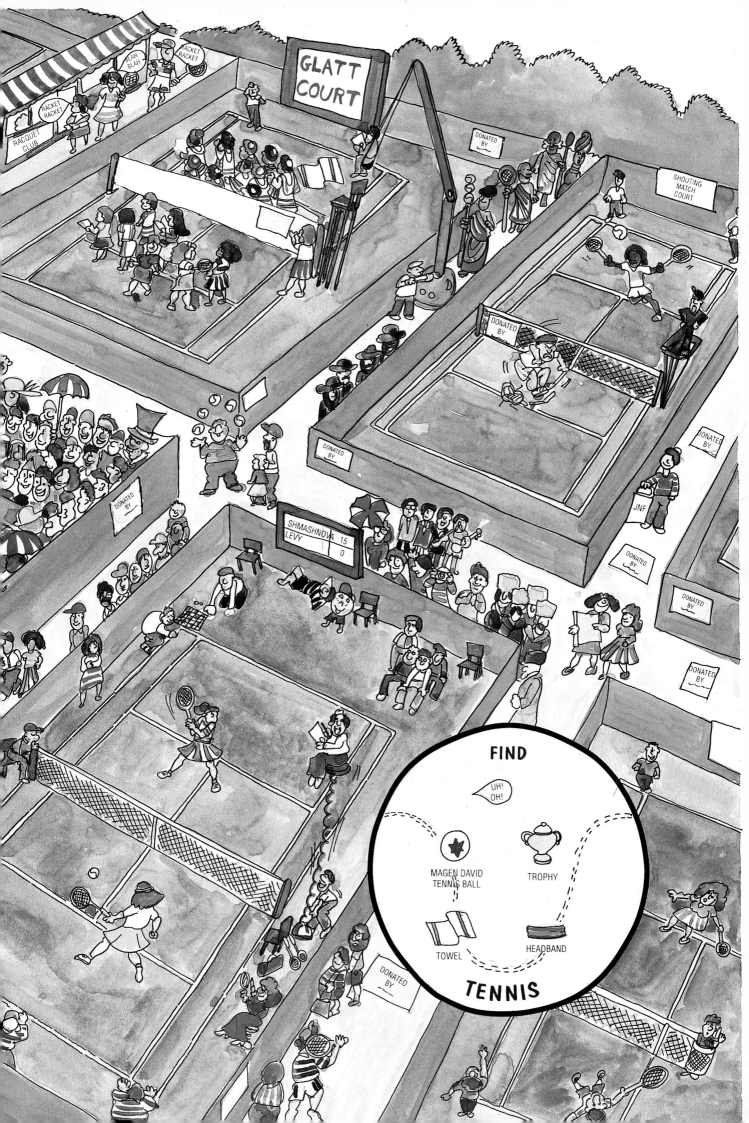

OLYMPICS

"It was the best of times, it was the worst of times." (Charles Dickens)

It was in 1972, at Munich, Germany that the Jewish people had their best — and worst — Olympic moments. Their best achievement was when Jewish swimmer, Mark Spitz, won seven medals. Their greatest sorrow was the murder of 11 Israeli athletes.

Mark Spitz is considered the best male swimmer. He was born in Sacramento, California and by age 12, he won almost every competition in his area. However, Sacramento was not the place to become a world-class swimmer, so Mark's parents moved to Santa Clara, California, where the best coaches and facilities are found.

At 15, Mark was already a champion in the freestyle and butterfly races. He won an amazing ten gold medals in the Maccabiah Games in Israel.

"I felt I could be the best in the world," he said. "Whatever I did, I was first."

Mark's achievements were incredible, but he had a higher goal — to be in the Olympics. Sure enough, he made the team and went to Mexico City for the 1968 Games. He was shocked by the anti-Semitism from team members.

"It was basic. I was called 'Dirty Jew' and 'Lousy Jew.' I was upset!"

Mark gathered his strength and won two gold medals, but for him that wasn't much.

"I learned the hard way. Don't talk — just swim. Let the records do the talking," he told his coach.

"Plus," he added, with a twinkle in his eye, "if you don't open your mouth, no water can get in."

After these Games, Mark practiced seven to ten hours a day. His parents came to the pool to bring him food. His father said, "Nothing else was important. He barely spoke to anyone. Winning was all that mattered."

Mark had the talent; now it was time to get his mind in shape.

"When you're a teenager, it's skill that counts. But the one who wins is the one who's tough up here," Mark said, pointing to his head. "All world-class athletes can swim."

It was the physical and mental combination that saw Mark through. At the 1972 Munich Games, he won an incredible seven gold medals — the most anyone had ever won at one Game. And every medal was a world record!

But Mark was not at the closing of the Games. He had been taken away by security after the massacre of the 11 Israeli athletes.

Palestinian terrorists had gotten past security into the Israelis' dormitory. They murdered two Jewish athletes and held nine others hostage. They told the German police that if they got a helicopter to take them away, they would release the hostages. At the airport, they bound the nine athletes and put them in the helicopter. However, before the terrorists could get away, the police opened fire. The cowardly terrorists threw hand grenades into the helicopter and killed the nine bound Israelis.

The world was outraged and there was a cry to cancel the Games. Nevertheless, in the end, the Olympic officials decided that the Games should go on.

But, this wasn't the first time Jews suffered at an Olympics. In 1936, the Games were also in Germany, Berlin this time. The Nazis had come to power three years before. It is well-known that under Adolf Hitler, the Nazis excluded Jews from all walks of life, including sports. The Nazis closed Jewish sporting clubs, expelled Jewish members of non-Jewish clubs and forbade Germans to play with Jews.

When the world discovered this, there was a movement to move the Games from Germany. But the German government *invited* the Jews to try out for the German teams (of course, none were accepted). After much controversy, the Olympic officials "turned a blind eye" to what was happening and let the Games take place in Berlin.

Two great Jewish runners were on the USA team: Marty Glickman and Sam Stoller. When it came to the final, most important track race, the Americans surprised everyone by keeping Glickman and Stoller on the sidelines.

They said it was purely a strategic decision, and since the USA won, the anti-Semitism could never be proved. But the fact was, they didn't want to "upset" their Nazi hosts.

There have been Jewish Olympians before and after the 1936 and 1972 Games in Germany. In the first years of the 20th Century, there were the Flatow brothers — Alfred and Felix — who won gold medals in gymnastics for Germany.

In 1924, at the Paris Olympics, English sprinter Harold Abrahams won the 100-meter race, the first and only Briton to capture such a title. His story was the basis for the award-winning movie, "Chariots of Fire."

In the 1984 Games, gymnast Mitch Gaylord won four gold medals; and Israeli judoists Yael Arad and Oren Smadja won silver and bronze medals in the 1992 Barcelona Games, and have done us proud in the 1996 Olympics.

But the world will always remember the 1972 Munich Games, when Jewish hopes were lifted to the heights by Mark Spitz — and dashed unmercifully to the ground by Palestinian terrorists.

At the 1996 Olympic Games, a special memorial was dedicated to mark the massacre at Munich.

BOXING

Until about two hundred years ago, boxing was an extremely brutal sport. Boxers were actually tied together at the waist with a cord whose length only allowed for one opponent to fall down while leaving the other one standing. There was no running and no hiding. Boxers just stood toe-to-toe and slugged it out until one dropped, and frequently died.

A boxer who helped change all that was a Jewish champion from England, named Daniel Mendoza. Mendoza lived in London about 200 years ago, around the time of the American Revolution. It might be said that he too was a revolutionary, not on the battlefield or in the halls of government, but in the boxing ring.

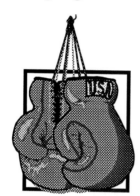

Mendoza invented a new way of fighting: the art of defensive fighting. It is the type of boxing we see today, where the fighters weave, bob and jab. They duck blows, fake blows and are constantly moving.

Mendoza's methods became so much a part of boxing that they were known as the "The Mendoza School" or "The Jewish School."

Mendoza was not a tall man. He was only 5-foot-7 and weighed 160 pounds, but his upper body, especially his chest, was well developed. He looked like he belonged in the ring.

Mendoza became such a popular fighter that he was given backing by the Prince of Wales. Associating boxing with royalty was good for the sport. Mendoza's rules for boxing also gave the sport some respectability.

Boxing continued to gain respectability, and a famous set of rules about boxing was published — The Marquis of Queensberry Rules. These rules were based on Mendoza's own book, "The Art of Boxing", and finally led boxing to be called "the gentlemanly art of self-defense".

Mendoza was proud of his Jewish heritage. He was known as "The Star of Israel" and he referred to himself as "Mendoza the Jew".

When Mendoza became a champion he set up a boxing school in Whitechapel, which is the neighborhood in London that he had come from, and instructed Jewish children how to defend themselves.

In the early 1900s it was very difficult for Jewish children to grow up in big cities like New York and Chicago. The road to acceptance wasn't easy. Other groups of immigrants didn't want the Jewish immigrants to move into their neighborhoods and take over the valuable space in their already cramped lives.

This time period in America was known as "The Golden Age of Jewish

Boxing." There were many fighters and some had colorful names and legends. They include: Harry "The Hairpin" Harris, Leach "The Fighting Dentist" Cross, Battling Levinsky, Ruby "The Jewel of the Ghetto" Goldstein, Al "The Bronx Beauty" Singer and perhaps the most poetic, "Slapsie" Maxie Rosenbloom.

The Jews learned to fight and to protect their turf. One of the best fighters was Barnet Rosofsky of Chicago's West Side, who later went on to become the boxing champ, Barney Ross.

Why would someone choose boxing? For Barney Ross, his decision was made the day his father, a grocery store owner, was gunned down in a robbery.

After his father died, his mother was unable to raise Barney and his three bothers and sister. The family split up. Barney and a brother went to live with a cousin, and Barney's two younger brothers and sister were sent to an orphanage.

A heartbroken Barney promised himself that he would one day reunite his family. Since he was good with his fists, he turned professional. Even before his father's murder, Barney had liked boxing. In fact, he had changed his name to Barney Ross, because he didn't want his mother to recognize his name on posters.

Not long afterwards, he found himself fighting for the lightweight championship. He won, and with that money, Barney was able to bring his brothers and sister back together again, and he even had enough money to have them cared for.

After Barney won the lightweight championship, he decided to fight in the next level weight, which is known as welterweight. He won that too, and for four years he held both crowns — the first boxer ever to do so.

But Barney Ross paid a heavy price for his championships.

The fast life got Barney into trouble. He gambled and drank away most of his money. He became an addict, and soon found himself penniless, and powerless in the ring. He was, however, successful in overcoming his addiction, and his story is told in a 1940s movie called "Monkey on My Back."

It's A Knockout!

FOOTBALL

Football is a complex sport that demands a lot of strategy. Most of the strategy revolves around the quarterback who calls the plays, directs each move and passes the ball. Because of all his power, he's called the "Field General." But it wasn't always that way. Sometimes, the quarterback didn't even start the play. When running backs stood about five yards behind the linemen, it was called the Single Wing Formation. One back would get the ball and the other three would block for him.

That's the way it used to be...

Then along came George Halas, coach and owner of the Chicago Bears. He was a pioneer in football strategy. Halas devised a new offense, the kind we know today, the T-Formation. In this setup, the quarterback stands behind the center, gets the ball and starts the play.

Halas needed a tough, intelligent quarterback to implement his new offense. That's where Jewish quarterback Sid Luckman came in. Sid was the star of his team at Columbia University, and also an excellent student. He was ready to go to graduate school until Halas spoke to him.

"Sid," he said, "You're the man I'm looking for. I need a quarterback with brains to run my offense. There'll be lots of different plays and you'll be in charge."

Sid wasn't sure. In those days professional football was still new and had many problems. But Halas made Sid an offer he couldn't refuse, and Sid joined the team in Chicago.

Chicago was far from home and Sid was lonely. Luckily, he was welcomed by the city's Jewish population. Sid said that the High Holy Days were the toughest.

Sid was invited to spend them with Chicago's rabbi. "I told him I wasn't an Orthodox Jew. He just smiled and said, 'Make sure you beat the Cardinals on Sunday.'"

Sunday was a major game between Chicago's two teams, the Bears and the Cardinals. For the Jews it was an important game since both quarterbacks were Jewish. The Cardinal's quarterback was Solly Sherman. Sid and Solly both played great games. Solly threw a touchdown and ran for another, but Sid was even better. He threw three touchdown passes and led the Bears to a big win. The next day Chicago newspapers wrote about "The Sid and Solly Show," and how they made the Jews proud.

"We were very happy," said the Chicago rabbi. "No matter which team came out on top, we were winners."

Another important player in football is the offensive lineman. His job is to block for the quarterback and open spaces for the players to carry the ball.

Jewish star Ron Mix was a famous lineman. He was a tackle for the University of Southern California and had to make a difficult decision when he entered professional football.

Just when he turned pro, a new league was recruiting players. It was called the American Football League (AFL), a rival to the more established National Football League (NFL). Ron received one offer from the Baltimore Colts of the NFL and a second from the Los Angeles Chargers of the AFL.

Ron's friends pushed Baltimore. "How do you know the other league will be here in a year?" they asked. But Ron thought he would get to play more with the new league, and joined the Los Angeles Chargers.

Ron was known for leading ball carriers and blocking everyone in his path. He once bowled over three defenders in one play and led his halfback to a touchdown. Ron was a big hit in the AFL.

Harris Barton is a lineman for the San Francisco 49ers. He is the only Jew in the NFL today. For years Harris protected quarterback Joe Montana from getting tackled.

"Why do you think Joe was so good?" Harris asks. "We made sure nobody got near him."

Jews have also been involved in coaching. The most famous Jewish coach is Marv Levy of the Buffalo Bills. Marv is known for two things: He developed the no-huddle offense, and his quarterback yelled out the play in code without a huddle. This makes for a very fast-moving game, and gives the defense less time to catch their breath.

Unfortunately, his Buffalo Bills lost four straight Super Bowls. But as he says, with a smile on his face, "Wait 'til next year."

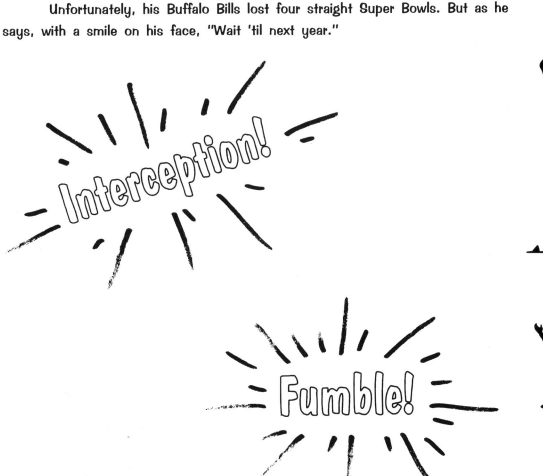

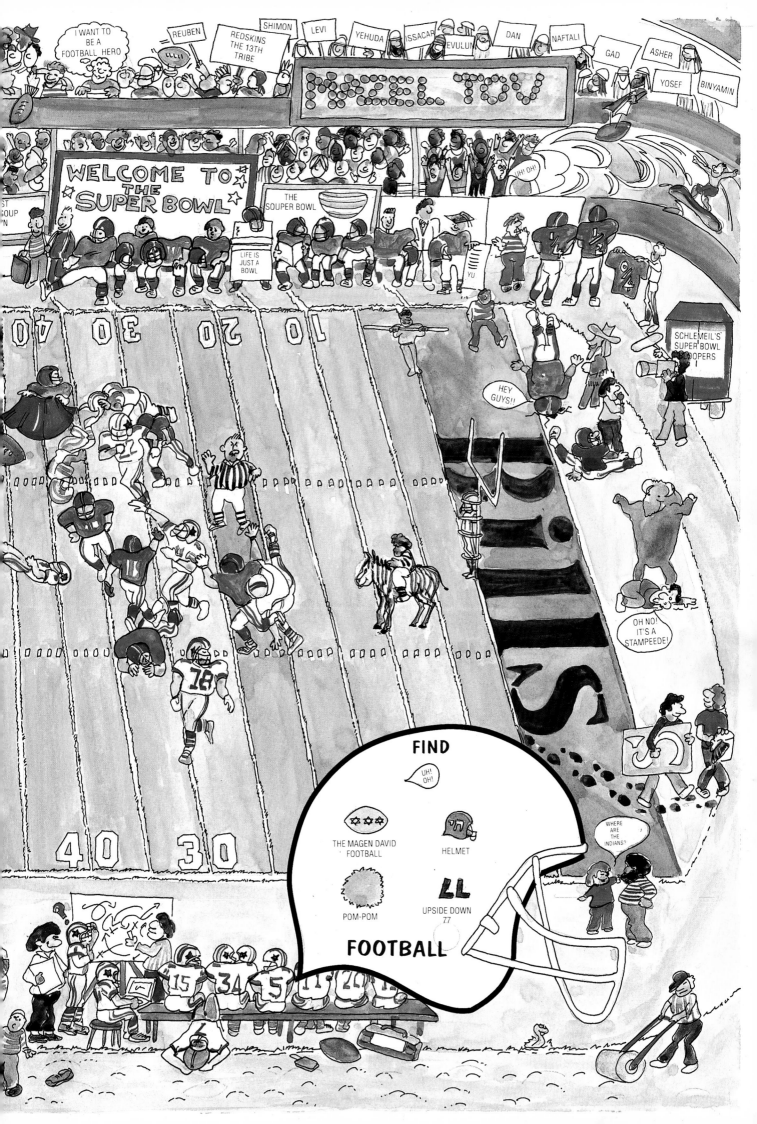

LACROSSE

You have to be tall to play basketball. You have to be big to play football. But in lacrosse, size doesn't matter. In fact, one of the best lacrosse players ever was five-foot-two. His name was Jerome Schneidman and he played lacrosse for Johns Hopkins University in Baltimore.

Lacrosse is a fast-moving game and only the best athletes can keep up. Jerome always thought he'd never play with the "big guys" but found that lacrosse was just the sport for him. Every morning before school, he would run three miles to get in shape, and practice hand-eye coordination by juggling tennis balls.

All this physical fitness helped Jerome excel in other areas as well. "When I got to school, I was so awake that I became a better student, too," he once said.

On the field, being short could even be an advantage. To play lacrosse, you have to keep the ball in the lacrosse stick and then shoot by flinging the stick forward and aiming the ball into the net. Meanwhile, the other team's defense man tries to stop you by blocking you or knocking the ball out of your stick by hitting it with his own.

Jerome discovered that being so small made it easier to move around the defenders. Some were so big that they would bend down to block him, and before they knew it, Jerome would dodge right past them. Once he made the front page of the newspaper by going through a defender's legs!

Another time, a defender tried to knock Jerome out of bounds. Jerome rolled the ball around him, stepped out of bounds, ran back inbounds behind the defender and picked up the ball. The defender got so confused that he fell over his own feet. Jerome kept on going.

His teammates nicknamed him *Ghost*, because of his "disappearing acts."

All the colleges with big lacrosse programs wanted Jerome. He even had offers from the Naval Academy. Jerome knew that the Academy had a height requirement and was amazed to discover that the coach had gotten the Academy to lower its minimum to five-foot-two just so Jerome could play.

But, in the end, Jerome chose Johns Hopkins. For four years, he was an All-American, and in his last year, he was the best player in the country. For a short guy, Jerome was a "big man on campus."

Lacrosse is not played professionally, so after college Jerome started to coach. He became the assistant coach at Johns Hopkins, and later, he became the Dean of Students.

When asked what kind of students he chooses to come to Johns Hopkins, he laughed and answered, "Students five-foot-two or smaller!"

The Lacrosse Hall of Fame, located in Baltimore, is full of Baltimore players, and like Jerome Shneidman, many are Jewish.

Another great Baltimore player was Dr. Joe Wilder. He went to the same high school as Jerome and was an All-American at Dartmouth College. Joe succeeded because of a simple discovery. As in most sports, lacrosse players are categorized as either right-handed or left-handed. An ambidextrous player has an obvious advantage: his opponent doesn't know which side he will throw from, or to which side he will run.

A natural righty, Joe practiced for hours to develop his left-handed lacrosse skills.

"I was so sore, I thought my left hand would fall off, but soon it got easier."

Joe's brother practiced with him patiently every day after school. "My brother lost his leg in a streetcar accident. He sat in his wheelchair and practiced with me. I owe everything to him," Joe admitted.

When defenders saw Joe coming with the stick in his left hand, they waited for him to switch to his right hand. But he never did. He shot with his left hand. "I wasn't the greatest natural athlete but I learned to shoot from both sides, and that's what made me an All-American."

After Dartmouth, Joe went to medical school. "When I watched doctors operating I noticed that they basically worked with one hand. "Sometimes, they had to move back and forth in surgery so they could always use the same hand. Since I could use both hands equally, I thought I'd be a great surgeon!"

Joe's a surgeon at New York University Medical School, and he teaches surgery. He tells his students, "Go to the park and learn to throw with your weak hand. Then come back and we'll learn some medicine."

Joe is also an accomplished painter. Not surprisingly, he likes to paint sports pictures.

"But," he says with a smile, "I only paint with my right hand."

The MACCABIAH GAMES

The Maccabiah Games, also called "The Jewish Olympics", are held every four years in Ramat Gan, near Tel Aviv in Israel. Since sports people come from all over the world to raise the flag of Jewish physical prowess, you may wonder — where did it all start?

Just over one hundred years ago, Theodore Herzl, the father of Zionism, changed Jewish sports forever. At a World Congress of Jews trying to return to Israel, Herzl told everyone how difficult life would be there. With swamps to drain, houses to build, and enemies to fight, the Jews would need not just brain power, but strength as well. He said that the Jews need to develop a "Judaism of Muscles" to get through the difficult times ahead.

When Herzl first urged the creation of Jewish sports clubs, he was opposed by almost everybody. But Herzl kept his idea alive, and all over Europe Jewish athletic clubs formed.

After a while, Jewish sportsmen wanted to test themselves against each other. "We must bring Jewish athletes together to compete," said Joseph Yekutieli, a Tel Avivian whose life was dedicated to the Maccabi movement.

At first, winter games were held in Belgium and Czechoslovakia, which brought together many skiers. But summer games were more exciting. Yekutieli convinced people in Israel that the summer games should be held there. The first games were held in 1932, and almost didn't get off the ground. The stadium was barely completed on time. Mosquitoes buzzed everywhere, and the humidity wore people out. Worst of all, there was hardly any money to stage the games.

Joseph and George Rubinovich, two brothers, came from America to participate. Joseph was a swimmer and George a runner.

"When we came," Joseph said, "I asked where the pool was, and the organizers laughed at me. 'Listen,' I told them harshly, 'I just came from a 15-day journey and I'm not in the mood for jokes.'"

The organizers pointed to the Mediterranean Sea and declared, "There is the pool." They had roped off 100 square yards, and called it a pool!

"It was the first pool I'd seen where you could get bitten by an octopus. I may laugh now, but then, I wondered how we'd survive."

When George went to practice for his track events, he saw that only half the track had an asphalt surface.

"Don't worry," the organizers said, "the course will be finished in time."

Joseph and George looked at the stadium. Stands were still being set up and grass was being put in place — barely one week before the official start.

"When camels brought in the cement, we looked at each other and then we *really* laughed," Joseph exclaimed.

"We finally got into the spirit, though," George recalls. "We were not only athletes, but pioneers. These were the first Jewish games in Israel and we were America's goodwill ambassadors. We were here to build a country, not just a sports stadium."

Somehow everything was finished on time and George and Joseph joined around 400 other sports people from 14 countries. At the opening ceremony, there was an impressive display of 1,500 gymnasts, and before the start 120 pigeons were released — ten for each of the 12 tribes.

In 1935, at the last Games before World War II, most of the German Jews decided to stay in Israel. Since they had defied Nazi orders by coming, and refused to fly their country's flag at the opening ceremony, it was safer not to go back.

Many Jews today also decide to stay, but not for the same reasons. They come for the first time during the Games and fall in love with the State of Israel.

"I met my wife, Leah, here," says Joseph. "She was a gymnast from Germany, and we met in the dining room."

The Rubinovichs stayed, and in the last Games, they had two grandchildren competing — like them — in gymnastics and swimming.

Joseph and Leah have raised four children and are the proud grandparents of 12.

"One for each of the 12 tribes," he laughs.

A Perfect 10!

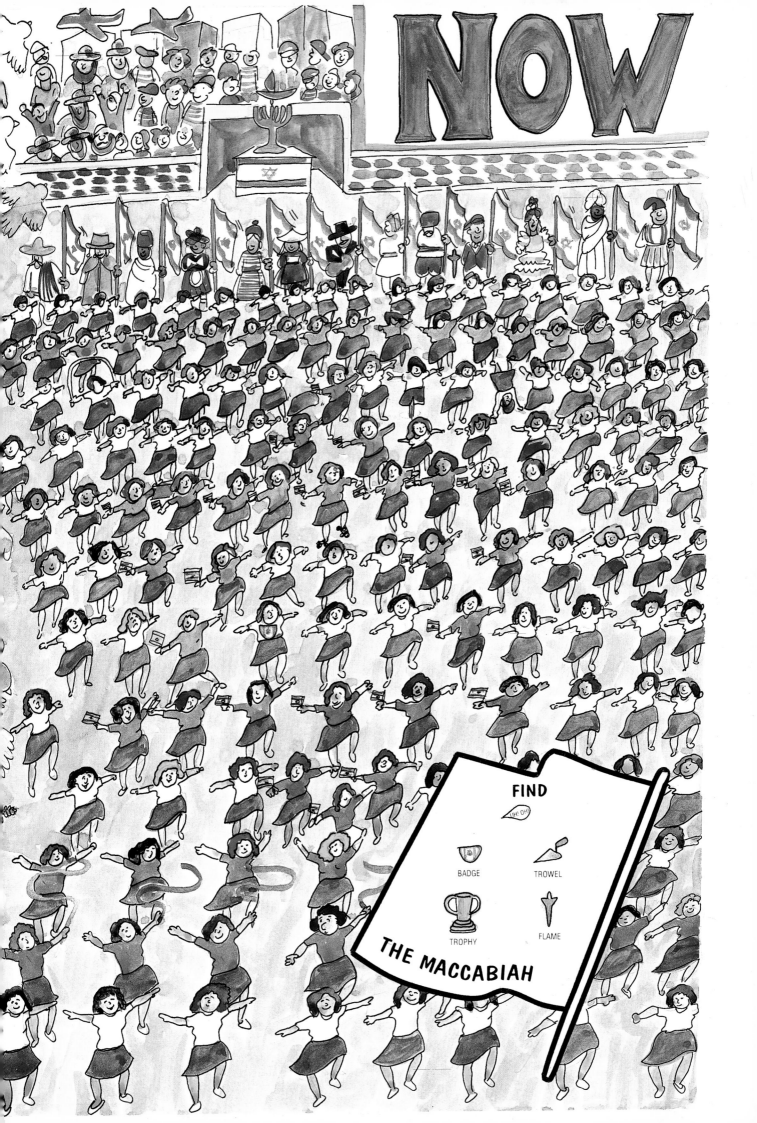